STEM Superstars

Shigeru Miyamoto

by Rachel Castro

NORWOOD HOUSE PRESS

Cover: Miyamoto has created famous video game characters.

Norwood House Press
Chicago, Illinois

For information regarding Norwood House Press, please visit our website at:
www.norwoodhousepress.com or call 866-565-2900.

PHOTO CREDITS: Cover: © Casey Curry/Invision/AP Images; © 7maru/iStockphoto, 9; © Barone Firenze/Shutterstock Images, 15; © Jae C. Hong/AP Images, 16; © Joy-Hung/Shutterstock Images, 5; © Miguel Riopa/AFP/Getty Images, 11; © Paul Sakuma/AP Images, 20; © Phil McCarten/Reuters/Newscom, 12; © portishead1/iStockphoto, 6; © skvalval/Shutterstock Images, 19

Hardcover ISBN: 978-1-68450-921-8
Paperback ISBN: 978-1-68404-459-7

Library of Congress Cataloging-in-Publication Data
Names: Castro, Rachel, author.
Title: Shigeru Miyamoto / by Rachel Castro.
Description: Chicago, Illinois : Norwood House Press, [2020] | Series: STEM Superstars | Audience: Grades: K to Grade 3. | Includes index.
Identifiers: LCCN 2018054270 (print) | LCCN 2018056955 (ebook) | ISBN 9781684044641 (ebook) | ISBN 9781684509218 (hardcover) | ISBN 9781684044597 (paperback)
Subjects: LCSH: Miyamoto, Shigeru, 1952---Juvenile literature. | Nintendåo Kabushiki Kaisha--Biography--Juvenile literature. | Nintendo video games--Design--History--Juvenile literature. | Video game designers--Biography--Juvenile literature.
Classification: LCC GV1469.32 (ebook) | LCC GV1469.32 .C37 2019 (print) | DDC 794.8092 [B] --dc23
LC record available at https://lccn.loc.gov/2018054270

319N–072019
Manufactured in the United States of America in North Mankato, Minnesota.

★ Table of Contents ★

Chapter 1

Early Life

Shigeru Miyamoto was born in Sonobe, Japan, in 1952. He did not have many toys. He had to make his own.

Miyamoto grew up in Sonobe, Japan. It is now named Nantan, Japan.

Drawing manga is very popular in Japan.

Miyamoto used wood and string to make puppets. He put on puppet shows. He also liked to draw. He drew **manga**.

Miyamoto grew up without a TV. He spent a lot of time outside. He liked exploring forests and caves nearby.

Some forests near Miyamoto's home have bamboo.

9

Chapter 2

Art to Design

Miyamoto wanted to be an artist. He thought everyone else was better at drawing. But he didn't let this stop him.

Miyamoto has always enjoyed drawing.

11

When Miyamoto joined Nintendo, the company had been making video games for two years.

Miyamoto studied **design**. He made toys. He brought these toys to a job **interview**. The interview was at Nintendo. Nintendo makes video games. He got the job.

Chapter 3

Video Games

Miyamoto made up characters for games. Then he got a chance to make his own game. He made *Donkey Kong*. It was very popular.

Donkey Kong is a large ape.

Mario is Miyamoto's most famous character.

He makes games with ideas from his life. His games *Super Mario Bros.* and the *Legend of Zelda* have caves and forests. They are ideas from his childhood.

Chapter 4

Finding a Story

Miyamoto likes to have stories in his games. Characters have adventures. Mario jumps, climbs, and explores.

Miyamoto's games take players on an adventure.

19

Miyamoto's video games have a **plot** like a book or movie. He changed video games forever. Miyamoto still designs video games today.

The Zelda games also helped make Miyamoto famous.

★ Career Connections ★

1 If you're interested in games, start by making your own games with what you have. You can use a deck of cards, LEGOs, puzzle pieces, or coins.

2 Play video games! If you come across a game you didn't enjoy playing, try to think of ways it could be better.

3 Once you're ready to learn about computer programming, use websites like Code.org. It has games and learning tools for kids. It even links to local schools that teach coding. Another website is MIT Media Labs Scratch Platform, where you can create 2-D games.

4 A local club or library may host a STEM Makerspace. There you can learn about robotics, coding, and more with other kids who like the same things.

5 Tell stories! Miyamoto's video games tell stories, like a book or movie. Write your own story and share it with friends and family.

★ Glossary ★

design (di-ZINE): To draw something that could be made.

flipbooks (FLIP-books): A book with a series of pictures; when the pages turn quickly, the pictures tell a story.

interview (IN-tur-vyoo): A meeting where someone is asked questions, often to get a job.

manga (MAYN-guh): Japanese comics.

plot (plot): A series of main events that create a story.

★ For More Information ★

Books

Kari A. Cornell. *Nintendo Video Game Designer Shigeru Miyamoto*. Minneapolis, MN: Lerner Publications, 2016. This book teaches kids about Miyamoto and how he changed video games.

Ben Hubbard. *How Coding Works*. Chicago, Illinois: Capstone, 2017. This book introduces coding to children.

Heather Lyons. *Programming Games and Animation*. Minneapolis, MN: Lerner Publications, 2018. This book teaches kids how games are designed.

Websites

Code.org

(https://code.org/) This website has courses to teach children coding and has listings for local classes.

Scratch

(https://scratch.mit.edu/) This website teaches kids the basics of coding with stories, games, and animations.

23

★ Index ★

★ About the Author ★

Rachel Castro is a Minneapolis-based writer. She holds degrees in English literature and creative nonfiction. In addition to writing for the educational market, she works for a public library and teaches creative writing.

24